MATCH!
THE BEST FOOTBALL MAGAZINE!

REAL MADRID
ANNUAL 2016

Written by Iain Spragg
Designed by Chris Dalrymple

Contents

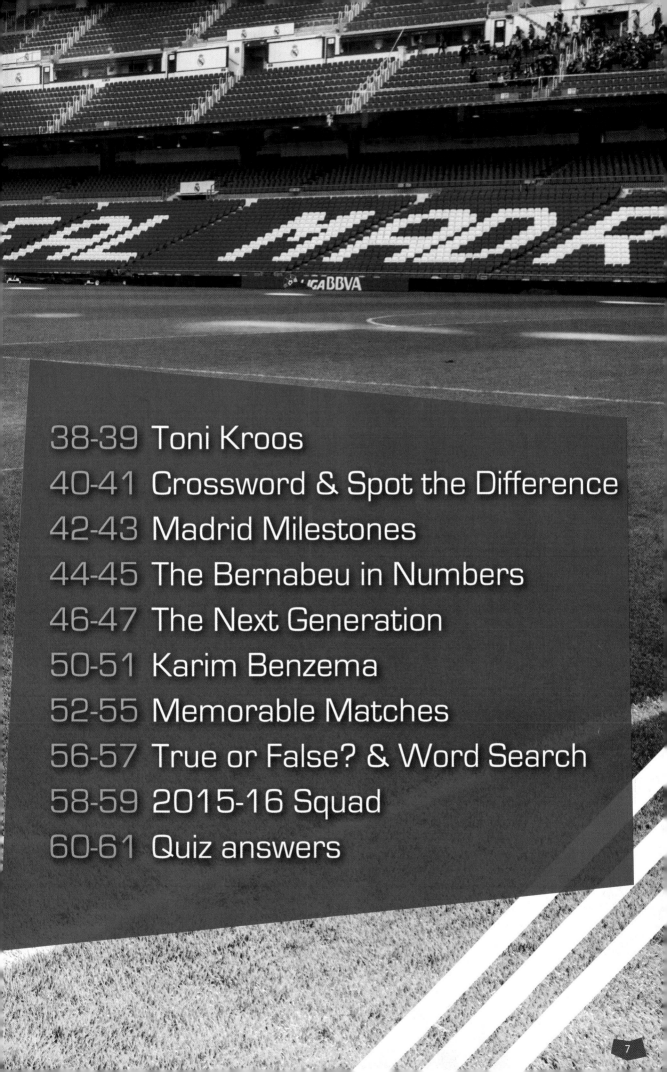

SEASON REVIEW 2014-15

Carlo Ancelotti's second and last season in charge at the Bernabeu saw the brilliant Los Blancos lift two more major trophies after his side's victories in the UEFA Super Cup in August and the FIFA World Club Cup in December.

Expectations at Real Madrid are always high and the team made sure they kicked off the new season in style, beating Sevilla 2-0 in the UEFA Super Cup thanks to two goals from Cristiano Ronaldo to claim the trophy for the first time since 2002.

The annual match between the reigning Champions League and Europa League champions was held in Cardiff a week before the start of La Liga and Ronaldo was in amazing form as the Portuguese superstar began his sixth season as a Madrid player with a bang.

His first goal came from a beautiful Gareth Bale cross from the left, sliding in at the far post to give Los Blancos a first-half lead, while his second came in the 49th minute when he slammed home an unstoppable left-footed drive which flew into the top corner.

Four months later the team headed to North Africa to play in the FIFA World Club Cup in Morocco and Ancelotti's side came home with more silverware after two superb victories to earn the title of the best club side on the planet.

Their first game was the semi-final against Mexican side Cruz Azul and Real were in the driving seat from the moment Sergio Ramos opened the

WINNERS
UEFA SUPER CUP 2014

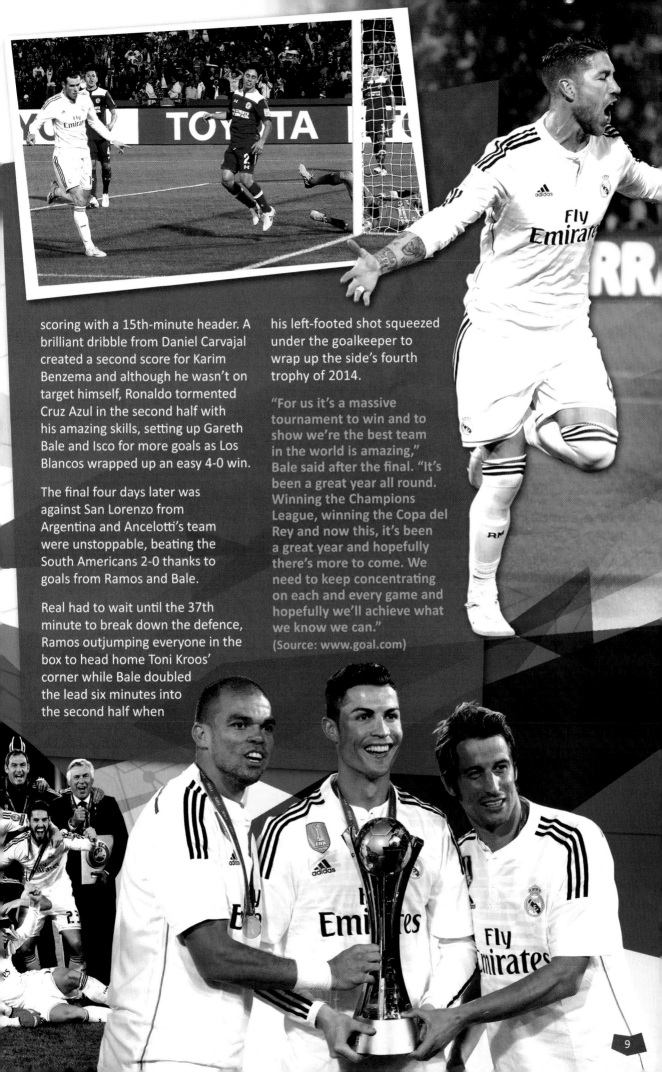

scoring with a 15th-minute header. A brilliant dribble from Daniel Carvajal created a second score for Karim Benzema and although he wasn't on target himself, Ronaldo tormented Cruz Azul in the second half with his amazing skills, setting up Gareth Bale and Isco for more goals as Los Blancos wrapped up an easy 4-0 win.

The final four days later was against San Lorenzo from Argentina and Ancelotti's team were unstoppable, beating the South Americans 2-0 thanks to goals from Ramos and Bale.

Real had to wait until the 37th minute to break down the defence, Ramos outjumping everyone in the box to head home Toni Kroos' corner while Bale doubled the lead six minutes into the second half when his left-footed shot squeezed under the goalkeeper to wrap up the side's fourth trophy of 2014.

"For us it's a massive tournament to win and to show we're the best team in the world is amazing," Bale said after the final. "It's been a great year all round. Winning the Champions League, winning the Copa del Rey and now this, it's been a great year and hopefully there's more to come. We need to keep concentrating on each and every game and hopefully we'll achieve what we know we can."
(Source: www.goal.com)

Real returned to Spain to begin their challenge for La Liga title and started off with a 2-0 win over Cordoba at the Santiago Bernabeu and as the season unfolded, the battle to be crowned champions became a two-way fight between Ancelotti's side and old rivals Barcelona.

The teams played each other twice in El Clasico with Real winning 3-1 in Madrid in October thanks to goals from Ronaldo, Pepe and Benzema. Barcelona took the points in the rematch at the Nou Camp in March and it was neck and neck between the two giants of Spanish football as the season reached its climax.

Real responded to the defeat in Barcelona by thrashing Granada 9-1 the following week with five goals from Ronaldo and in their last 10 league games, Los Blancos won nine and drew one. It was a great finish to the season but not quite enough to overhaul Barcelona for top spot and after 38 matches, the Catalans were champions, just two points ahead of Ancelotti's team.

It was a similar story as Real tried to defend their Champions League crown. Six wins from six in the group stage saw the side easily qualify for the knockout phase of the competition and they made no mistake in the Last 16, beating German side Schalke 5-4 on aggregate.

Their quarter-final against city rivals Atletico Madrid was more tactical and tense and in the 180 minutes of play over the two legs there was only goal, on-loan striker Javier Hernandez scoring in the 88th minute of the second game at the Bernabeu to dramatically send Los Blancos into the semi-finals.

Italian champions Juventus stood between Real and a place in the final but Ancelotti's side paid a heavy price for a 2-1 defeat in the first leg in Turin. The second leg at the Bernabeu eight days later started well when Ronaldo scored from the penalty spot early in the first half but Juventus equalised after the break and a 1-1 draw was not enough to keep Real in the competition they had won 12 months earlier.

"It's hard," admitted Ramos after the final whistle. "The team fought but now we have to say goodbye. We thought we had done enough with the goal but we let it slip."
(Source: www.nydailynews.com)

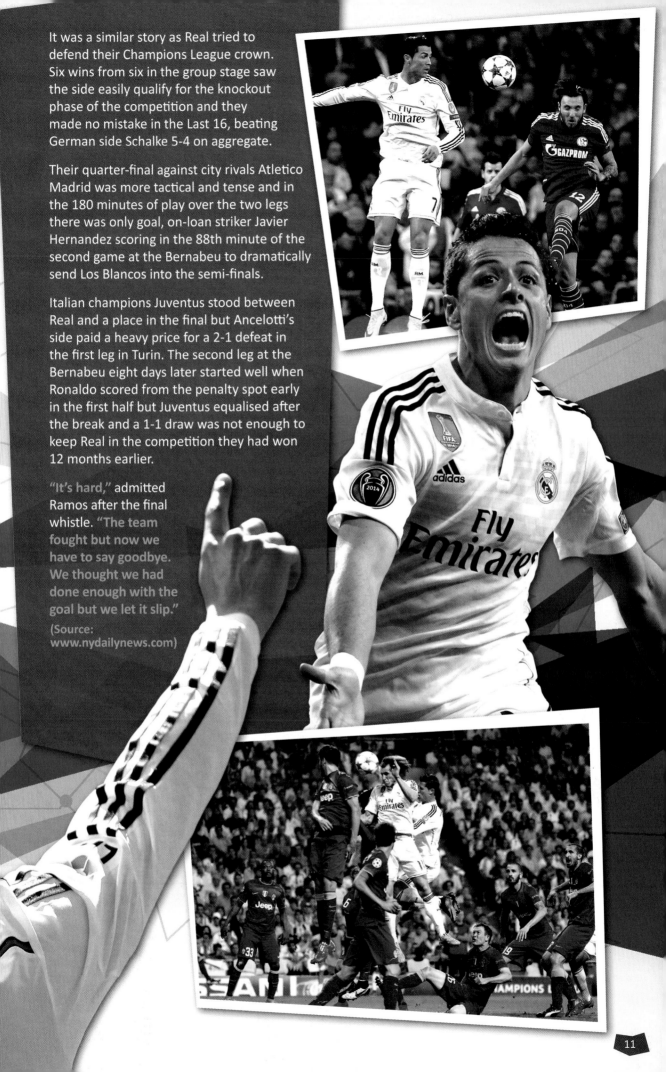

2015
S CUP Australia
Audi

International
CHAMPIONS CUP
Australia

PRESENTED BY
Audi

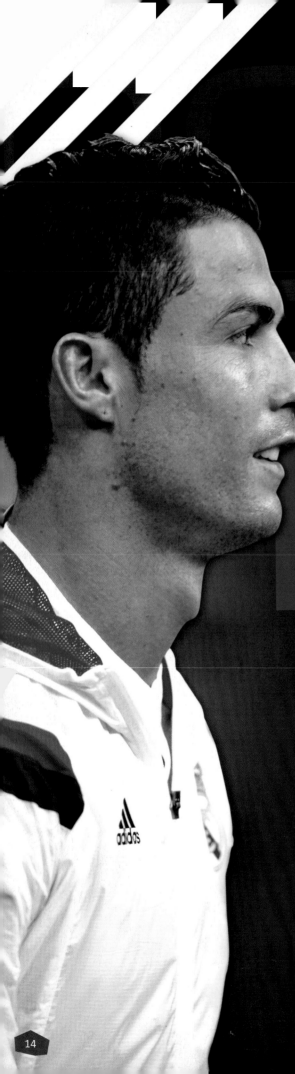

Madrid Heroes
CRISTIANO RONALDO

Crowned the best player on the planet in 2015 for a third time in his phenomenal career, the unstoppable Portuguese superstar is now poised to become Los Blancos' all-time leading goalscorer.

When Cristiano Ronaldo signed for Real Madrid in 2009 from Manchester United in what was then a world record £80million deal, some people questioned whether any player could be worth such a massive fee. After six record-breaking seasons at the Santiago Bernabeu, he has made the deal look like a bargain.

The story of Ronaldo's incredible Real career began with a goal against Liga de Quito in the Peace Cup and after registering his best ever season in front of goal in 2014-15, scoring 61 times in just 54 games to take his Madrid tally to 314, he now has Raul's club record of 323 firmly in his sights.

Ronaldo's greatest strength is simply that he has no weaknesses in his game. Physically powerful, lightning quick and incredibly fit, he has a thunderbolt shot, brilliant dribbling skills and is a huge threat in the air. His long-range passing is deadly and he can play anywhere across the pitch.

His first five seasons in Spain were awesome but 2014-15 saw the superstar claim even more club and La Liga records, kicking off the campaign in August with a double against Sevilla to win the UEFA Super Cup for Los Blancos.

His hat-trick against Celta Vigo in December in his 178th La Liga appearance saw him become the fastest player in the competition's history to reach the 200 goal milestone. It was also his 23rd league treble, another La Liga record. Later the same month he was at his brilliant best in Morocco as Real won the FIFA Club World Cup for the first time.

In April he scored his 300th goal for Los Blancos in a 2-0 victory at Rayo Vallecano while the following month his strike against Juventus at the Bernabéu saw him become the joint top goalscorer in Champions League history with 77. He finished the season with a hat-trick against Getafe, his eighth of the league campaign and another record for La Liga.

It was no surprise that his brilliant form brought Ronaldo a host of individual accolades. In January he won the FIFA Ballon D'Or – awarded to the world's best player – for a third time while his 61 goals also saw the Portuguese pick up the European Golden Shoe for a record fourth time in his career. His 10 goals in the Champions League made him the tournament's top scorer for a remarkable third year running.

The star has helped Real claim seven major trophies since quitting England for Spain and after his most prolific season for the club in 2014-15, Ronaldo and his goals look certain to bring even more silverware to the Bernabeu.

REAL MADRID

RONALDO

7

Legends of The Bernabeu

The ten greatest players to wear the famous white shirt of Real Madrid.

IKER CASILLAS

Years: 1999-2015
Appearances: 725

Honours: La Liga (5), Copa del Rey (2), Spanish Super Cup (4), Champions League (3), UEFA Super Cup (2), FIFA Club World Cup, Intercontinental Cup (2).

The brilliant Spain goalkeeper joined Los Blancos as a nine-year-old in 1990 and during his amazing Madrid career he won every domestic, European and world trophy on offer.

HUGO SANCHEZ

Years: 1985-1992

Appearances: 283 (208 goals)

Honours: La Liga (5), Copa del Rey, Spanish Super Cup (3), UEFA Cup.

Los Blancos' top scorer for five consecutive seasons, the Mexican striker boasted an incredible strike rate during his time at the Bernabeu and helped the club win 10 major trophies.

RAUL

Years: 1994-2010

Appearances: 741 (323 goals)

Honours: La Liga (6), Spanish Super Cup (4), Champions League (3), UEFA Super Cup, Intercontinental Cup (2).

No-one has made more appearances for Real than Raul, who captained the side for seven glorious seasons and scored in two Champions League finals.

ZINEDINE ZIDANE

Years: 2001-2006

Appearances: 227 (49 goals)

Honours: La Liga, Spanish Super Cup, Champions League, UEFA Super Cup, Intercontinental Cup.

Voted the FIFA World Player of the Year during his Bernabeu career, the magical French midfielder scored a famous, spectacular winning goal in the 2002 Champions League final.

ALFREDO DI STEFANO

Years: 1953-64

Appearances: 510 (418 goals)

Honours: La Liga (8), Copa del Rey, Champions League (5), Intercontinental Cup.

The star player of Madrid's golden era in the 1950s, the fantastic forward from Argentina scored in five European Cup finals in a row to earn his place in the Real record books.

ROBERTO CARLOS

Years: 1996-2007

Appearances: 527 (68 goals)

Honours: La Liga (4), Spanish Super Cup (3), Champions League (3), UEFA Super Cup, Intercontinental Cup (2).

The Brazilian full-back was loved by the fans for his fearless attacking style and thunderbolt left-foot shot, earning a place in the UEFA Team of the Year in both 2002 and 2003.

GUTI

Years: 1995-2010

Appearances: 542 (77 goals)

Honours: La Liga (5), Spanish Super Cup (4), Champions League (3), UEFA Super Cup, Intercontinental Cup (2).

The long-serving midfielder is 10th on the all-time list of appearances for Madrid and lifted 15 major trophies during his glittering Bernabeu career.

FERENC PUSKAS

Years: 1958-1967

Appearances: 262 (242 goals)

Honours: La Liga (5), Copa del Rey, Champions League (3), Intercontinental Cup.

La Liga's top scorer in four separate seasons, the Hungarian striker was a key player in the famous Madrid side that dominated Spain and Europe in the 1950s and 1960s.

FERNANDO HIERRO

Years: 1989-2003

Appearances: 601 (127 goals)

Honours: La Liga (5), Copa del Rey, Spanish Super Cup (4), Champions League (3), UEFA Super Cup, Intercontinental Cup (2).

Voted Europe's best defender in 1998, Hierro could play in the back four or midfield and enjoyed 14 amazing seasons with Los Blancos, winning three Champions League titles.

RONALDO

Years: 2002-2007

Appearances: 177 (104 goals)

Honours: La Liga, Spanish Super Cup, Intercontinental Cup.

The Brazilian superstar spent less than five seasons in Madrid but still banged in a century of goals, top scoring for Los Blancos as they were crowned La Liga champions in 2002-03.

Meet the New Boys

All you need to know about Real Madrid's big summer signings

JESUS VALLEJO

KIKO CASILLA

One of the hottest young talents in European football, Vallejo is a brilliant central defender who has already made a big impact in Spain with his performances during the 2014-15 season for Real Zaragoza.

Madrid made their move for Vallejo in the summer, signing the teenager on a six-year deal. He will spend the 2015-16 campaign back at Zaragoza on loan but looks set for a long and successful career at the Santiago Bernabeu.

Vallejo broke into the Zaragoza first team in August 2014 with a debut against Recreativo de Huelva and by the end of the season he had been appointed captain, just three months after celebrating his 18th birthday.

The defender has also been a big hit with the Spanish junior teams. A graduate of the Under-16 and Under-17 squads, he captained the Under-19 team in the UEFA Championship in Greece this summer, taking the side all the way to the final where they beat Russia 2-0 to become champions.

"I've talked to Marco Asensio, my team-mate with Spain Under-19s. He told me he will help me at Madrid whenever I need it."

(Source: www.as.com)

Casilla began his professional career at the Bernabeu as a teenager, playing in the Second Division with the club's reserves for two seasons but could not force his way into the first team and left for Espanyol in 2007 on a free transfer.

The 6ft 3ins goalkeeper spent eight years at Espanyol, making more than 100 league appearances for the club and made a reputation for himself as a brilliant shot-stopper and a commanding presence in the air. No keeper made more saves in La Liga than Casilla in both the 2013-14 and 2014-15 seasons.

He rejoined Real in the summer when he signed a five-year deal with his first club. Los Blancos paid £4.3 million to bring him back to the Bernabeu.

An Under-19 and Under-21 cap, he finally forced his way into the senior Spain side when he was handed his international debut in November 2014 from the bench in a friendly against world champions Germany.

"My aim is to work hard and be a success at Real Madrid."

(Source: www.realmadrid.com)

CASEMIRO

DANILO

The Brazilian midfielder actually signed for Real in 2013 but he spent the 2014-15 season on loan at Porto and returns to the Santiago Bernabeu for the 2015-16 campaign hoping to nail down a regular place in Rafa Benitez's star-studded first team.

A versatile and physically strong player, Casemiro first made his name in Brazil with Sao Paulo. He made over 100 appearances for the club and in 2012 he was part of the side which won the Copa Sudamericana, one of South American football's biggest tournaments.

A few months later he signed for Los Blancos and after finding his feet in the Madrid B team, he was rewarded with a first team debut in 2013 against Real Betis in La Liga.

His successful loan spell in Portugal saw the midfielder help Porto reach the quarter-finals of the Champions League.

Casemiro broke into the Brazil team as a teenager when he played against Argentina in 2011 and like new Bernabeu team-mate Danilo, he was part of the Brazilian squad that lifted the Under-20 World Cup and the Under-20 South American Championship in the same year.

> ## "Coming back to Madrid has been a gift."
> (Source: www.realmadrid.com)

A right full-back with brilliant power and great pace and the ability to join the attack, the exciting Brazil international joined Los Blancos in the summer in a £22 million, six-year deal from Portuguese club Porto.

Danilo began his professional career with the América Mineiro side in Brazil but was quickly snapped up by South American giants Santos. After two impressive seasons he moved to Europe when he was signed by Porto, winning two Portuguese league titles and two Super Cups with the team in just three seasons. In total he made 139 appearances and scored 13 goals for the club.

At international level, the defender won both the Under-20 World Cup and the Under-20 South American Championship with Brazil in 2011 and then made his debut for the senior team later in the year against old rivals Argentina.

He also picked up a silver medal with the Samba Boys at the 2012 Olympic Games in London, playing four times and finding the back of the net in the group stage win over New Zealand.

> ## "Joining the best club in the world is a dream come true."
> (Source: www.realmadrid.com)

TOP 10 GOALS

Los Blancos scored an incredible 162 goals in all competitions in the 2014-15 season. Here are the top ten strikes from their net-busting campaign.

Cristiano Ronaldo v Cordoba (La Liga, 25 August)

The first La Liga game of the new season and Ronaldo wasted no time in supplying the fireworks, scoring with a long-range drive from 45 yards out that beat the keeper and glanced off the post.

Gareth Bale v Real Sociedad (La Liga, 31 August)

The Welshman scored his first goal of the campaign with a magical bit of skill, nutmegging a bemused Sociedad defender on the edge of the box with a brilliant spin and collecting Luka Modric's pass before firing home a deadly left-footed shot which rocketed into the bottom left corner.

Karim Benzema v Basel (Champions League, 16 September)

A stunning team goal, Real's fifth of the match, which was created by a brilliant one-two between Ronaldo and the French striker, who then struck a deadly shot with his weaker left foot that screamed past the Basle keeper and went in off the crossbar.

Javier Hernandez v Deportivo (La Liga, 20 September)

Real smashed eight past Deportivo and the pick of the bunch was Hernandez's spectacular effort from 30 yards out, the on-loan Mexican striker hitting an instant volley after coming off the bench, which almost burst the net.

Cristiano Ronaldo v Levante (La Liga, 18 October)

Midfielder Isco led the charge from deep inside the Real half before finding Ronaldo wide on the left. The striker cut inside the first two defenders, leaving them for dead, and once he had powered his way into the area, he unleashed an unstoppable shot that smashed into the top corner.

James Rodriguez v Granada (La Liga, 1 November)

The £71 million new boy scored twice in a 4-0 win over Granada to send Real top of La Liga and his first strike was unbelievable, picking up Benzema's clever flick and hitting a first-time volley with the outside of his right boot that sailed over the keeper.

Gareth Bale v Espanyol (La Liga, 10 January)

Ronaldo is the man who takes most of Real's free-kicks but Bale made the most of his chance against Espanyol, sending his superb 40-yard effort over the wall, curling past the stranded keeper and into the back of the net off the inside of the left post.

Karim Benzema v Real Sociedad (La Liga, 31 January)

There seemed no danger when Benzema collected the ball on the left of the Sociedad area but his one-two with Isco created space and the French striker sent the Bernabeu faithful wild with an amazing, first-time effort that curled beautifully into the back of the net.

Marcelo v Schalke (Champions League, 18 February)

The Brazil defender scored four goals in the 2014-15 season and his best came in Europe against Schalke, the full-back lashing home a thunderbolt effort from outside the area that left the keeper clutching thin air.

James Rodriguez v Malaga (La Liga, 18 April)

A goal that showcased all the young Colombian's talents, it began with a one-two with Isco and featured another with Ronaldo before Rodriguez took aim and slammed the ball into the back of the net despite the Malaga keeper getting a hand to his shot.

Madrid Heroes

GARETH BALE

The Welsh wing wizard has been a huge hit at the Santiago Bernabeu since h[is] world record switch from Spurs to Spain two years ago, helping Los Blancos win four major finals.

When Gareth Bale signed for Real Madrid from Tottenham Hotspur in the summer of 2013 in a £85 million deal, making him football's most expensive player ever, he told the fans he was coming to the club to lift trophies.

The Welshman had been in sensational form in England for Spurs but had yet to pick up a winner's medal in his career. The move to the Bernabeu changed all that, and in the space of two seasons Bale had played a key part in the side's successes in the Copa del Rey, the Champions League, the UEFA Super Cup and the FIFA Club World Cup.

His first taste of glory came in April 2014 when Real faced arch rivals Barcelona in the final of the Copa del Rey in Valencia. The game was deadlocked at 1-1 with five minutes to play until Bale paid off a big part of his massive transfer fee with a sensational solo winner, picking up the ball in his own half and outpacing the helpless Barca defence.

found the back of the net again in the final as Los Blancos beat Argentinian opponents San Lorenzo 2-0 to finish the tournament as joint top scorer.

His performances in La Liga for the club were equally impressive. His first league campaign saw Bale grab 15 goals in just 27 appearances while he notched up 13 more in the 2014-15 season.

Bale's most eye-catching strength is his incredible pace but he has great technical ability and a deadly left foot from set-pieces. His amazing fitness also means he can play at top speed for the whole 90 minutes.

The Welshman signed a six-year deal with Los Blancos when he arrived at the Santiago Bernabeu in 2013 and after two hugely successful seasons in Spain, the Real faithful can look forward to four more years of turbo-charged action from their new hero.

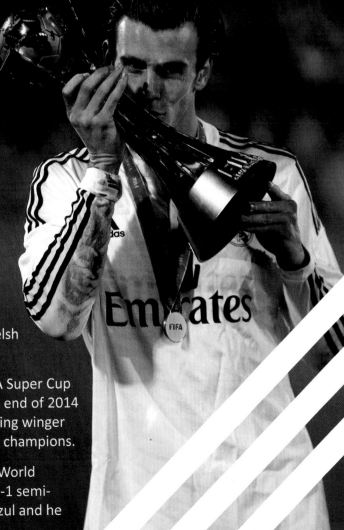

He was on target again the following month as Los Blancos were crowned champions of Europe for a record 10th time. The Champions League final against Atletico Madrid went to extra-time but it was brilliant Bale who put Real ahead with a back post header. Madrid eventually won 4-1 and the Welsh star had a second big title to his name.

In August Real beat Sevilla in the UEFA Super Cup to give Bale a trophy treble but by the end of 2014 it was four winner's medals for the flying winger as the team were crowned world club champions.

Bale was sensational in the FIFA Club World Cup, held in Morocco, scoring in the 4-1 semi-final victory over Mexican side Cruz Azul and he

The BIG
Real Madrid Quiz

20 questions to test your knowledge of the world-famous Bernabeu club.

1. Real Madrid hold the record for the most La Liga titles. How many times have they been league champions?

2. In what year was the club's Santiago Bernabeu stadium opened?

3. The 2014-15 season was Cristiano Ronaldo's best yet for the club. How many goals did he score?

4. Which player holds the record for the most games for Madrid with 741 appearances?

5. How many followers did the club's official Twitter account have by July 2015?

6. Real last won the Champions League in 2014. Which Spanish side did they beat in the final?

7. Midfielder James Rodriguez is named after which famous British film character?

8. Madrid made history in 2009 when they became the first club to spend £50 million on a player. Who was it?

9. From which Premier League club did Madrid sign Gareth Bale for £85 million in 2013?

10. Midfielder Luka Modric plays international football for which country?

11. What is the English translation of the word 'Real' in the club's name?

12. Bernabeu boss Rafa Benitez used to be in charge of which two English clubs?

13. Which non-Spanish player holds the record for the most club appearances?

14. How old was Norwegian midfielder Martin Odegaard when he became Real's youngest ever player on debut in May 2015?

15. Real's fixture against which club is known as 'El Derbi Madrileño' in Spanish?

16. Which company supplies the official Real Madrid kit?

17. How many La Liga titles did Miguel Munoz win during his record-breaking 14-year stint as Real manager?

18. Which defender scored Madrid's first goal in the 2014 Champions League final?

19. How many back-to-back league titles did Real win in the 1980s?

20. To which team did Real sell Angel di Maria in 2014 for a club record fee of £60 million?

Answers on p60.

Spot
the Ball

Can you spot which is the real ball?

Answer on p60.

In The Hot Seat
RAFA BENITEZ

After Real narrowly missed out on La Liga title and the Champions League crown in 2014-15, Los Blancos turned to local boy Rafa Benitez to bring the trophies back to the Bernabeu this season.

There was a tear in Rafa Benitez's eye when he was unveiled as Real's new manager in June 2015. It was, though, a tear of joy as he realised his lifelong dream of taking charge of the team he had supported as a boy and the club he has always loved.

Benitez was born and raised in Madrid. He played for the club's junior teams as a teenager and he also began his coaching career at the Bernabeu. When it was confirmed he would replace Carlo Ancelotti, Los Blancos' new boss was a picture of pride.

"I am coming home," he said. "It is a special day and a very emotional one. I've been working for many years to achieve success and return home, which was always one of my aims. I promise work and dedication, I hope that things go well and that we win titles, that the team plays well and that we can return the confidence that has been placed in us. I have a very good team of staff by my side and hopefully everything we hope for will come true."
(Source: www.mirror.co.uk)

Benitez's love affair with the Los Blancos began when he joined the club at the age of 13. He never broke into the first team but did make nearly 500 appearances for the reserves and when he was forced to retire in 1986 aged 26 with a serious knee injury, he decided to turn to coaching.

He spent nine years working with the Real youth teams and reserves before finally leaving his hometown club to gain more experience but, even though he didn't know it at the time, he would be back at the Bernabeu in 20 years' time.

His big breakthrough came in 2002 when he steered Valencia to La Liga title. He repeated the trick in 2004 and after being voted the UEFA Manager of the Year, Benitez was one of the hottest properties in European football.

His next stop was England when he became the Liverpool manager. The Spaniard stayed at Anfield for six years and won four trophies, most famously beating AC Milan in the final of the Champions League in 2005 to see the Reds crowned the kings of Europe for a fifth time in the club's history.

Since then Benitez has taken charge at Inter Milan, Chelsea and Napoli and, although his stints at all three clubs were short, he won trophies with each team to underline his reputation as a man who knows exactly how to get his hands on silverware.

RAFA BENITEZ'S MANAGERIAL RECORD

1993-1995	Real Madrid B
1995-1996	Valladolid
1996	Osasuna
1997-99	Extremadura
2000-01	Tenerife
2001-04	Valencia
2004-10	Liverpool
2010	Inter Milan
2012-13	Chelsea
2013-15	Napoli

RAFA BENITEZ'S TROPHIES

La Liga	2001-02, 2003-04
UEFA Cup	2004
FA Cup	2006
Community Shield	2006
Champions League	2005
UEFA Super Cup	2005
Italian Super Cup	2010, 2014
Europa League	2013
FIFA Club World Cup	2010
Italian Cup	2014

Inside
Real Madrid

Incredible Los Blancos trivia and fun facts

According to a 2015 study backed by FIFA, Gareth Bale is the world's fastest footballer with the ball at his feet. The Welsh winger, who once ran the 100 metres as a teenager in 11.4 seconds, was clocked dribbling at 23 mph.

Unlike many modern footballers, Cristiano Ronaldo doesn't have any tattoos. That's because he gives blood regularly and people who have been inked are sometimes not allowed to donate because of fears about infection.

A recent report named Madrid as the world's richest club for the 10th year in a row. The study showed the club generated an incredible £460 million in revenue during the 2013-14 season.

Toni Kroos' younger brother Felix is a also a professional footballer and plays for German Bundesliga side Werder Bremen.

Los Blancos' first ever manager was an Englishman called Arthur Johnson who played for the club as a striker before coaching the team between 1910 and 1920.

Striker Karim Benzema comes from a big family and has eight brothers and sisters.

Real Madrid became the first team in Spain to play in shirts with numbers on the back. They first ran out with numbered shirts in the city derby against Atletico Madrid in...

Real started wearing their famous white shirt in 1902 after copying the kit of a London amateur team called Corinthians.

In 2011 Los Blancos released an album on iTunes called 'Legends' which included a remix of the official Madrid anthem 'Himno del Real Madrid'.

Growing up in Croatia in the 1990s, midfielder Luka Modric was forced to flee his home because of the civil war in the country.

By July 2015, the official Real Madrid Twitter feed had 16.5 million followers. The club's Facebook page had received more than 83 million Likes.

Los Blancos are one of the three teams who set up the first football league in Spain. They are also one of only three teams never to have been relegated from La Liga.

Defender Pepe does a lot of charity work and last year paid for nine tonnes of food to be distributed in one of the poor neighbourhoods in Madrid to make sure no-one was hungry at Christmas.

Even though his first name is pronounced 'Hamez', James Rodriguez was named after the famous movie secret agent James Bond.

El Clasico

A fixture that boasts more than 100 years of incredible history, games between the superstars of Real Madrid and Barcelona are huge events which capture the imagination of football fans all over the world.

When it comes to sporting rivalry, it doesn't get any bigger than El Clasico. An amazing 400 million people from across the planet tuned in to watch the match between the two teams in La Liga in March 2015 and the Santiago Bernabeu is always a complete sell-out when Barca travel to Madrid.

The history of the fixture goes back to 1902 when the sides first faced each other in a friendly in the capital and ever since that game, the two biggest clubs in Spain have been locked in a fierce battle for trophies and titles.

The first competitive meeting of the duo was in 1916 when they were drawn against each other in the semi-finals of the Copa del Rey but the rivalry reached new heights in 1929 when La Liga was launched and what has become an annual battle to be crowned Spanish champions began.

Los Blancos are currently ahead of Barca in the all-time list of league titles with 32 triumphs to 23 for the Catalan side.

The world-famous fixture has produced some classic matches over the years. Madrid's biggest win is their 11-1 defeat of Barca in a cup match back in 1943, whilst one of Real's most important recent victories against their old rivals came in 2012 when Cristiano Ronaldo scored a late winner away at the Nou Camp to seal a 2-1 success, a result which helped Los Blancos seal the championship.

Such is the massive popularity of the match that in 2010 a film was released called 'El Clasico: More Than A Game', an hour-long documentary shot in the two biggest cities in Spain looking at the long and explosive history of the fixture.

Winners of the games are not always crowned champions of La Liga but it is always viewed as disaster by the fans if their side is beaten in El Clasico.

WHAT THEY SAY ABOUT EL CLASICO

"Madrid against Barca is a match we all love to play. Football lovers all over the world stop when there is a Clasico."

Jose Mourinho (Real Madrid manager, 2010-2013)
(Source: www.tribalfootball.com)

"It is the biggest game on earth at club level. It is crazy to think how many people stop to watch this game. You always say to your friend, where are you watching El Clasico? I can only compare it to the World Cup final or European Cup final."

Thierry Henry (Barcelona striker, 2007-2010)
(Source: www.skysports.com)

"It is the biggest match in football. There's a lot of rivalry between Liverpool and Manchester United, certainly, and Liverpool and Everton, but I've never seen rivalry of this standard."

Steve McManaman (Real Madrid winger, 1999-2003)
(Source: www.goal.com)

"It's not just any other game, it never is. If you win, it makes you feel great. El Clasico is always a battle in footballing terms. You have to be the best in everything to win."

Andres Iniesta (Barcelona captain)
(Source: www.theguardian.com)

EL CLASICO IN NUMBERS

170 – League matches between the two clubs since the first meeting in February 1929.

71 – Madrid victories over Barca in La Liga.

278 – Goals scored by Los Blancos against Barcelona in the league.

33 – Players who've represented both clubs during their career.

18 – Goals scored by Alfredo di Stefano for Real in El Clasico, a club record in the fixture.

2 – Cristiano Ronaldo goals in the two El Clasicos of 2014-15.

228 – Total competitive matches between the two sides up to the end of the 2014-15 season.

Los Blancos had **92** wins to **88** for Barcelona with **48** draws.

Madrid Heroes
TONI KROOS

A World Cup winner in Brazil in 2014 with Germany, the midfielder signed for Real four days later and in his first season underlined his world-class credentials with a series of superb performances for Los Blancos.

When Toni Kroos arrived at the Santiago Bernabeu in July 2014, he became the ninth German player in Real's history to wear the famous white shirt. He was following in the footsteps of great players like Paul Breitner, Bernd Schuster and Uli Stielike and, after just one year in Spain, Kroos looks set to become another German legend in Madrid.

Known for his amazingly accurate passing, his long-range shooting and his ability to create space and chances for team-mates, Kroos spent the first seven years of his senior career with German giants Bayern Munich, winning the Bundesliga title three times.

That success built his reputation as a top-class midfielder but it was Kroos' performances for Germany in the World Cup that really put him up among the best players on the planet. The playmaker scored twice as the Germans demolished Brazil 7-1 in the semi-final and he was on the pitch for the full 120 minutes in the final as the team beat Argentina 1-0 in extra time.

No-one provided more assists than Kroos in the tournament, setting up team-mates for goals four times in Brazil to showcase his creative skills.

His debut for Real just one month later was a cracker, starting the move that led to Cristiano Ronaldo's second goal as Los Blancos began the season with victory over Sevilla in the UEFA Super Cup.

His dazzling displays for both club and country in 2014 did not go unnoticed and by the end of the year he had picked up a long list of accolades which included nominations in the FIFA World Cup Dream Team, the UEFA Team of the Year and the FIFA World XI. In 2015 he added a place in the 2014-15 Champions League Team of the Season to his incredible collection of awards.

The future in Spain is bright for Kroos and with his irresistible mixture of power and vision, technical ability and athleticism, he could become the greatest ever German international to play for Real Madrid.

It was the start of a hugely impressive first year in Madrid. Kroos had joined a star-studded Real squad but it was proof of his immediate impact at the club that the star missed just two of Los Blancos' 38 La Liga fixtures, scoring his first goal in November in a 5-1 win over Rayo Vallecano.

The German was also a key player as Real were crowned the best club team on the planet in December. Kroos started both Madrid matches in the FIFA Club World Cup in Morocco, setting up Sergio Ramos' headed opening goal in the final with a superb corner and unlocking the defence in the build-up to Gareth Bale's second.

The Massive
Madrid Crossword

ACROSS

3. Brazilian defender who made 527 appearances for the club between 1996 and 2007. (7,6)

6. Team Real beat in 2014 in the final of the Champions League. (8,6)

8. Last club managed by Rafael Benitez before taking the Madrid job. (6)

11. Madrid's current kit supplier. (6)

13. Former England captain who played for Los Blancos between 2003 and 2007. (5,7)

15. Number of goals scored by Los Blancos in their victory over Granada in La Liga in April 2015. (4)

16. Colour of the team's world famous shirts. (5)

17. Costa Rican goalkeeper who made six appearances in La Liga in 2014-15. (6,5)

18. Italian team beaten by Real in the 1998 Champions League final. (8)

20. Title of the digital album of songs released by the club in 2011. (7)

DOWN

1. Country in which Madrid lifted the FIFA Club World Cup for the first time in 2014. (7)

2. Country of Bernabeu superstars Cristiano Ronaldo and Pepe. (8)

4. French striker who scored more than 100 goals for Los Blancos since 2009. (7)

5. Real Madrid manager between 2013 and 2015. (5,9)

7. Name given to the star-studded Madrid side of the early 2000s. (3,10)

9. Spanish phrase given to Real's famous fixture against arch rivals Barcelona. (2,7)

10. Scorer of the winning goal in the final of the Copa del Rey in 2014. (6,4)

12. Real's German 2014 World Cup winner. (4,5)

14. Goals scored by Real in 1943 in their record victory against Barcelona. (6)

19. Number of times Los Blancos have been crowned European club champions. (3)

Answers on p60

Spot the
Difference

Study both photographs below and see if you can spot the 11 differences.

Answers on p61

Madrid Milestones & Records

The players and managers who've set new milestones during their Bernabeu careers.

RECORD-BREAKING RAUL

The former Bernabeu hero holds the distinction as both the club's top goalscorer and the man to have made the most appearances for Los Blancos. The striker found the back of the net an incredible 323 times in 741 games during his 16 seasons in Madrid. A total of 228 of those goals came in La Liga while the legendary forward scored 66 in European matches.

EUROPEAN SERVANT

Raul holds the record for the most Madrid appearances but Iker Casillas played more European games for the club. The goalkeeper featured in a record 155 Continental matches for Real between 1999 and 2015, winning the Champions League three times.

STEFANO'S STAMINA

Bernabeu legend Alfredo Di Stefano was a remarkable talent but he was also a great athlete and he holds the club record for the most consecutive league games played. Between September 1953 and February 1959 the star didn't miss a La Liga fixture, an incredible run of 171 matches.

FOREIGN LEGION

Brazil full-back Roberto Carlos spent 11 hugely successful seasons at the Bernabeu and his 527 appearances is a club record for a player from outside Spain. His 370 La Liga games is also a record for a non-Spanish player.

SUPERB SANTILLANA

No-one has made more appearances for Madrid in the Copa del Rey than striker Carlos Santillana. The Spain international spent 17 years with the club and notched up 84 games in the competition.

THE MARVEL OF MUNOZ

Los Blancos have had many world-class managers in their history but the most successful is Miguel Munoz. The Madrid-born coach was in charge at the Bernabeu between 1960 and 1974 and collected 15 trophies. His incredible haul was nine La Liga titles, two Copa del Rey trophies, the European Cup twice and the Intercontinental Cup. Munoz is also the longest-serving Real manager ever with 604 games in charge.

A SEASON TO REMEMBER

Cristiano Ronaldo is closing fast on Raul's record of 323 goals for Real but the Portuguese superstar already holds the distinction as the most prolific Madrid player ever in a single season, finding the back of the net an unbelievable 61 times in just 54 games during the 2014-15 campaign.

TEENAGE TALENT

The youngest player to represent Real in a competitive match is Norwegian midfielder Martin Odegaard who was just 16 years and 157 days old when he made his first team debut in La Liga against Getafe in May 2015. The youngest ever scorer for the club in a competitive match is midfielder Alberto Rivera who was only 17 years and 114 days old when he netted for Los Blancos against Celta Vigo in 1995.

SIX-GOAL SALVO

Only two players have scored six goals in a match in Madrid history. The first to record a double hat-trick was Jose Maria de Benguria in 1927, the second Ferenc Puskas in 1961. Both players set their milestones in Copa del Rey matches. Seven different players have scored five in a league game, the most recent Cristiano Ronaldo when he bagged five as Real hammered Granada 9-1 in 2015.

QUICKFIRE SCORE

The quickest goal in Real history was scored back in 1994 in La Liga when Chile striker Ivan Zamorano found the back of the net after just 12 seconds against Sevilla.

BIG-MONEY DEAL

Madrid have been involved in some of the biggest transfer deals ever and they became the first club in football history to pay more than £50 million for a player when they signed Brazil midfielder Kaka from AC Milan in 2009 in a record-breaking £56 million deal.

The Santiago Bernabeu In Numbers

Everything you need to know about the world-famous home of Real Madrid

1947
Year in which the first ever game was played at the Bernabeu. Madrid beat Portuguese club Belenenses 3-1 in a friendly.

2007
Year in which Real Madrid played their 1000th match at the Bernabeu – a league match against Levante.

85,454
Current matchday capacity of the stadium.

65
Goals the team scored at their home ground in 19 La Liga matches during the 2014-15 season.

4
Games during the 1982 FIFA World Cup the ground hosted, including the final between West Germany and Italy.

4
European Cup finals the ground has hosted. The first saw Los Blancos beat Fiorentina 2-0 while the stadium also staged the finals of 1969, 1980 and 2010.

60,000
Fans who were inside the stadium in 2014 to watch The Rolling Stones as part of their '14 On Fire' tour.

1955
Year in which the club officially changed the name of the stadium from the Estadio Chamarten to the Santiago Bernabeu in honour of the Madrid president.

328
Millions of pounds the club will spend upgrading the Bernabeu over the next few years.

105
Length of the pitch in metres. It is 68 metres wide.

1997
Year in which the Bernabeu became an all-seater stadium.

2
Goals Spain scored against the Soviet Union at the Bernabeu in 1964 to win the final of the European Championships.

80,000
Number of fans who packed the stadium in 2009 to witness the official unveiling of Cristiano Ronaldo as a Madrid player.

4
Zones into which the ground is divided – Fondo Norte (North Side), Fondo Sur (South Side), Lateral (East Side), and Preferencia (West Side).

124,000
Record attendance at the stadium when Los Blancos played Fiorentina in 1957.

1957
Year in which Los Blancos played their first ever game under floodlights at the ground.

32
Goals scored by Ronaldo at the ground in all competitions during the 2014-15 season.

11
Goals Madrid scored at the ground against Elche in 1960. The 11-2 win is still the club's record victory in La Liga.

2008
Year in which midfielder Guti scored for Madrid against Numancia at the Bernabeu, the club's 5000th goal in La Liga.

The Next Generation

Meet the young Real Madrid players hoping to become the new superstars at the Santiago Bernabeu.

MARTIN ODEGAARD
DOB: 17 December 1998

The attacking midfielder is already an international footballer after making his senior debut for Norway in a friendly against the United Arab Emirates in August 2014 at the age of 15, becoming the youngest player to represent his country. He signed for Los Blancos from Norwegian club Strømsgodset in January 2015 and, after playing for the Madrid reserve team, he was handed his first team debut in May when he came off the bench in the 58th minute to replace Cristiano Ronaldo in a 7-3 win against Getafe, setting a new record as the club's youngest ever debutant in a competitive match. Odegaard is a brilliant technical player with great pace and a powerful shot.

ALVARO MEDRAN
DOB: 15 March 1994

The Spanish midfielder enjoyed a breakthrough season with Madrid in 2014-15, forcing his way into the first team, scoring his first goal for the club and making five appearances in total. His debut came in La Liga against Levante in October, replacing Luka Modric, while his goal came in the Champions League in December against Ludogorets Razgrad after coming on for Gareth Bale in the 83rd minute. Often compared to first team star Isco, the Under-21 international is a stylish playmaker and will spend the 2015-16 season on loan at Getafe to develop his game.

DIEGO LLORENTE
DOB: 16 August 1993

Born in Madrid, Llorente joined the Real youth system at the age of nine and, after working his way up through the ranks, made his first-team debut as a second-half substitute for Alvaro Arbeloa against Osasuna in May 2013. Capped by the Spain Under-20 side, the youngster is a strong central defender who is good in the air and boasts good pace. He made one appearance for the first team in 2014-15, coming on as a substitute in Los Blancos' 5-0 win over Cornella in December in the Copa del Rey.

JAVIER MUNOZ
DOB: 28 February 1995

A Spain Under-19 international, the attacking midfielder is small but hugely gifted and blessed with great vision and has been with the club since he joined the Madrid Academy in 2006 as an 11-year-old. Munoz has progressed quickly through Los Blancos' junior ranks, making 28 league appearances for the reserve team in 2014-15, before getting his opening shot of first team football in December when he came off the bench to replace James Rodriguez in the side's 5-0 defeat of Cornella at the Bernabeu in the Copa del Rey, a debut described as "assured" by manager Carlo Ancelotti.

JACK HARPER
DOB: 28 February 1996

Born in Malaga to Scottish parents, the teenager has already been dubbed the 'Scottish Ronaldo' and signed a five-year deal with Madrid in 2012. A tall, left-footed forward with a brilliant first touch and incredible technical ability, Harper is yet to break into the Real reserve team but has already represented Scotland at Under-17 and Under-19 level as well as starring for Los Blancos in the UEFA Youth League in 2014-2015, scoring three goals in six group stage matches.

MARCO ASENSIO
DOB: 21 January 1996

Signed from Mallorca in late 2014, Asensio is a winger with incredible dribbling skills and ability to control the ball in tight spaces. Capped by Spain at Under-16, Under-17 and Under-19 level, he spent the second half of the 2014-15 season back at Mallorca on loan, playing second division football. Currently on loan to RCD Espanyol.

Madrid Heroes

KARIM BENZEMA

One of the most deadly and naturally gifted goalscorers in world football today, the brilliant French marksman is the spearhead of the Real Madrid attack.

Every big club dreams of a striker who can consistently score 20 goals or more a season. Such players are rare in the modern game but in Karim Benzema Los Blancos have a forward who has repeatedly proved he can do it at the highest level.

Benzema arrived at the Santiago Bernabeu back in 2009 from French club Lyon. It cost Real £25 million to sign the 21-year-old and although his goals had helped Lyon win four French league titles, no-one knew if he'd make the grade in La Liga.

The Frenchman's first year in Spain was quiet as the youngster found his feet in a new country but in the five seasons that have followed Benzema has been a revelation, scoring at least 20 goals for Madrid in each campaign.

His breakthrough came in 2010-11 when he found the back of the net 26 times in 48 appearances but the following season was even better as he banged in 32 goals in 52 games as Los Blancos were crowned La Liga champions for the 32nd time in the club's history.

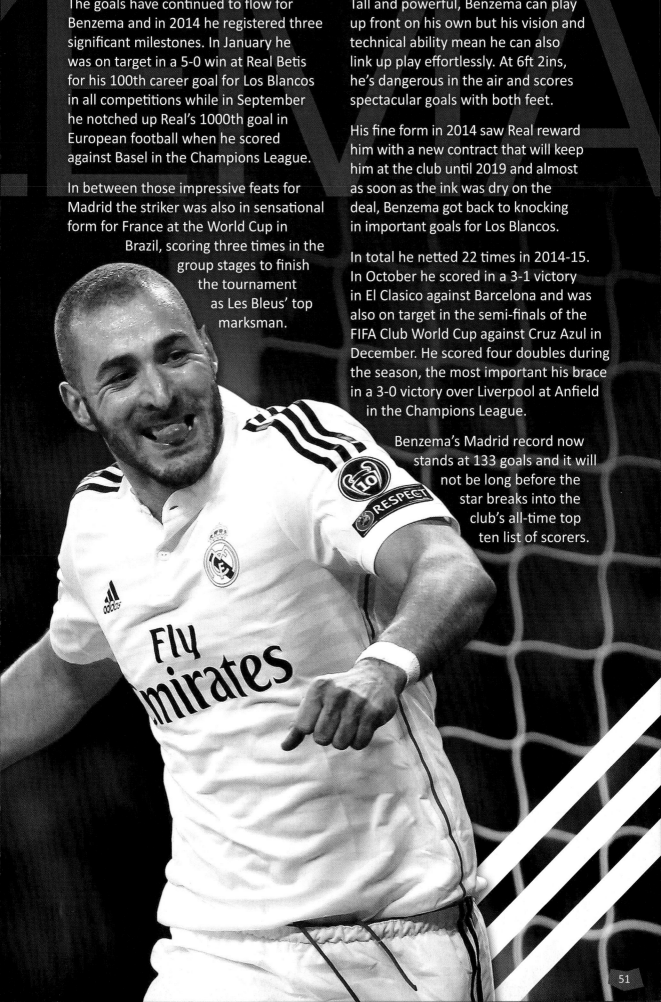

The goals have continued to flow for Benzema and in 2014 he registered three significant milestones. In January he was on target in a 5-0 win at Real Betis for his 100th career goal for Los Blancos in all competitions while in September he notched up Real's 1000th goal in European football when he scored against Basel in the Champions League.

In between those impressive feats for Madrid the striker was also in sensational form for France at the World Cup in Brazil, scoring three times in the group stages to finish the tournament as Les Bleus' top marksman.

Tall and powerful, Benzema can play up front on his own but his vision and technical ability mean he can also link up play effortlessly. At 6ft 2ins, he's dangerous in the air and scores spectacular goals with both feet.

His fine form in 2014 saw Real reward him with a new contract that will keep him at the club until 2019 and almost as soon as the ink was dry on the deal, Benzema got back to knocking in important goals for Los Blancos.

In total he netted 22 times in 2014-15. In October he scored in a 3-1 victory in El Clasico against Barcelona and was also on target in the semi-finals of the FIFA Club World Cup against Cruz Azul in December. He scored four doubles during the season, the most important his brace in a 3-0 victory over Liverpool at Anfield in the Champions League.

Benzema's Madrid record now stands at 133 goals and it will not be long before the star breaks into the club's all-time top ten list of scorers.

Memorable Matches

The top ten greatest games in the history of the world-famous Spanish giants.

Barcelona

BARCELONA 1 REAL MADRID 2
La Liga, 21 April 2012

Madrid were out for revenge after losing to Barca at the Bernabeu in December and they got it at the Nou Camp with a famous win that effectively sealed the 2011-12 La Liga title for Jose Mourinho's side. Sami Khedira's opener was cancelled out by Alexis Sanchez but Real sealed the all important three points when Cristiano Ronaldo went around the keeper to stun the Nou Camp into silence.

REAL MADRID 4 STADE DE REIMS 3
European Cup Final, 13 June 1956

Los Blancos are the most successful side in the history of European club football and they began their domination in 1956 after a stunning victory over French side Stade de Reims. Legendary forward Alfredo Di Stefano opened the scoring in Paris in the 14th minute and although Reims surged into a shock 3-2 lead, Real got their hands on the famous trophy when striker Hector Rial grabbed a dramatic late winner.

REAL ZARAGOZA 1
REAL MADRID 7
La Liga, 12 September 1987
Madrid began the 1987-88 season with a bang, beating Cadiz 4-0 and then Sporting Gijon 7-0 in their opening two league games, and they continued their dazzling form with a landslide 7-1 victory at Real Zaragoza. Real didn't score until the 30th minute but two goals from legendary Bernabeu striker Emilio Butragueño helped Los Blancos set a new club record for their biggest win away from home en route to being crowned La Liga champions.

REAL MADRID 7 EINTRACHT FRANKFURT 3
European Cup Final, 18 May 1960
An amazing fifth victory in the final on the bounce, Real's crushing defeat of the Germans in Glasgow was the pick of the bunch. No club has ever scored more goals in a European Cup final as Los Blancos destroyed the Frankfurt defence, Di Stefano helping himself to a hat-trick at Hampden Park while Hungarian hero Ferenc Puskas scored four.

VALENCIA 0
REAL MADRID 3
Champions League Final, 24 May 2000
The first final to feature two clubs from the same country, Real's eighth success in the competition was also Vincente Del Bosque's first trophy as Madrid manager. A first half header from Fernando Morientes put Real in the driving seat while a stunning volley from England winger Steve McManaman after the break was the pick of the goals. Striker Raul put the icing on the cake after 75 minutes to cap a brilliant Real performance.

Memorable
Matches

REAL MADRID 5 PENAROL 1
Intercontinental Cup, 4 September 1960

The first ever match-up between the champions of Europe and South America, the first leg in Uruguay had finished goalless but Madrid ran riot in the second leg in Spain two months later to earn the title of the best club side in the world. The writing was on the wall for Penarol after just two minutes when Puskas opened the scoring and it was all over for the visitors by half time as Los Blancos surged into a 4-0 lead.

BARCELONA 0 REAL MADRID 4
Copa del Rey Final, 29 June 1974

Real put their arch rivals to the sword in the Vicente Calderon stadium in front of 48,000 fans to record one of their greatest wins in El Clasico. Spain striker Santillana got the ball rolling with a fifth-minute goal while long-serving Real midfielder Pirri completed the scoring late in the second half as Los Blancos wrapped up their 12th Copa del Rey crown.

DEPORTIVO LA CORUNA 2 REAL MADRID 8
La Liga, 20 September 2014

Carlo Ancelotti's side scored an incredible 118 La Liga goals in 2014-15 and eight of them came away at Deportivo as the team equalled the club record for the biggest win away from home. Not for the first time Ronaldo was the star of the show with a superb hat-trick while Bale and Javier Hernandez both chipped in with a brace. James Rodriguez's stunning volley made it eight as Real swept to a crushing win.

Deportivo La Coruna

Atletico Madrid

REAL MADRID 4 ATLETICO MADRID 1
Champions League Final, 24 May 2014
The Madrid faithful had been waiting 12 years for their side to claim a 10th European crown and their side didn't let them down when they faced city rivals Atletico in Lisbon. The final went into extra-time with the two teams locked at 1-1 after 90 minutes but Los Blancos then ran riot with scores from Gareth Bale, Marcelo and Ronaldo to strengthen Real's status as the most successful club side in European football.

SAN LORENZO 0 REAL MADRID 2
FIFA Club World Cup Final, 20 December 2014
Goals from Sergio Ramos and Bale against their Argentinian opponents completed a famous win which saw Los Blancos recognised as the best team on the planet. The victory sealed Real's fourth major trophy of 2014 and was also the team's 22 win on the bounce in all competitions, a new club record.

San Lorenzo

True or False?

Can you tell fact from fiction with these Real Madrid teasers?

1. The very first El Clasico match between Real Madrid and Barcelona was played in 1929.

2. Los Blancos were relegated from La Liga for the first and only time in their history in 1961.

3. Cristiano Ronaldo was born in Lisbon, the capital of Portugal.

4. Real manager Rafa Benitez has a degree in physical education.

5. Real were the first team in Spain to wear shirts with numbers on the back.

6. Four different Madrid stars have been crowned the FIFA World Player of the Year.

7. Real have won the Champions League nine times.

8. Real were originally called Madrid Football Club.

9. The Santiago Bernabeu has hosted the final of the Champions League three times.

10. Real signed Cristiano Ronaldo from Manchester City in 2009.

11. Real were voted the FIFA Club of the 20th Century.

12. Gareth Bale is the first Welshman to play for Real Madrid.

13. The record crowd for a match at the Santiago Bernabeu is 110,000.

14. In 2005 the club released a film called Real, The Movie.

15. During the 1925-26 season, the team wore black shorts instead of white for the only time in the club's history.

Answers on p61

Word Search

Find the 20 Real Madrid stars past and present hidden in the grid.

```
X  C  D  T  W  S  E  T  N  E  I  R  O  M  Z
B  E  N  Z  E  M  A  K  F  E  O  T  M  O  F
M  D  O  B  O  K  X  R  M  L  N  N  J  R  G
P  N  R  D  R  Q  O  B  P  S  E  A  W  A  Y
B  H  R  O  A  D  J  W  K  A  U  Z  R  V  N
E  I  O  Z  E  G  M  G  V  L  G  A  Y  A  B
C  S  Q  E  R  J  L  K  G  L  A  M  G  N  V
K  P  S  S  M  O  G  A  E  I  R  O  M  N  Q
H  S  G  N  A  K  D  N  S  S  T  R  J  A  N
A  A  K  A  K  N  A  R  M  A  U  A  M  C  O
M  K  K  L  D  D  C  V  I  C  B  N  R  R  C
L  S  G  C  I  B  R  H  K  G  G  O  R  T  R
Q  U  G  Z  M  Z  T  L  E  M  U  E  G  Y  C
F  P  P  U  R  D  U  A  L  Z  I  E  M  K  L
R  O  N  A  L  D  O  N  K  H  W  P  Z  T  T
```

Answers on p61

Beckham   Morientes
Benzema   Puskas
Butragueno   Rodriguez
Cannavaro   Ronaldo
Casillas   Salgado
Hierro   Sanchez
Kaka   Seedorf
Kroos   Varane
Laudrup   Zamorano
Modric   Zidane

57

Real Madrid Squad 2015-16

GOALKEEPERS

Keylor Navas
Born: 15 December 1986
Country: Costa Rica
Signed: August 2014
Appearances: 11
Goals: 0

Kiko Casilla
Born: 2 October 1986
Country: Spain
Signed: July 2015
Appearances: 0
Goals: 0

DEFENDERS

Sergio Ramos
Born: 30 March 1986
Country: Spain
Signed: September 2005
Appearances: 445
Goals: 55

Pepe
Born: 26 February 1983
Country: Portugal
Signed: July 2007
Appearances: 285
Goals: 12

Raphael Varane
Born: 25 April 1993
Country: France
Signed: June 2011
Appearances: 117
Goals: 6

Alvaro Arbeloa
Born: 17 January 1983
Country: Spain
Signed: July 2009
Appearances: 228
Goals: 6

Dani Carvajal
Born: 11 January 1992
Country: Spain
Signed: June 2013
Appearances: 87
Goals: 2

Fabio Coentrao
Born: 11 March 1988
Country: Portugal
Signed: July 2011
Appearances: 100
Goals: 1
(currently on loan to Monaco)

Marcelo
Born: 12 May 1988
Country: Brazil
Signed: January 2007
Appearances: 320
Goals: 23

Nacho
Born: 18 January 1990
Country: Spain
Signed: Academy
Appearances: 57
Goals: 1

Danilo
Born: 15 July 1991
Country: Brazil
Signed: July 2015
Appearances: 0
Goals: 0

MIDFIELDERS

Toni Kroos
Born: 4 January 1990
Country: Germany
Signed: July 2014
Appearances: 55
Goals: 2

Lucas Silva
Born: 16 February 1993
Country: Brazil
Signed: January 2015
Appearances: 9
Goals: 0
(currently on loan to Marseille)

Casemiro
Born: 23 February 1992
Country: Brazil
Signed: January 2013
Appearances: 27
Goals: 0

Isco
Born: 21 April 1992
Country: Spain
Signed: June 2013
Appearances: 106
Goals: 17

James Rodriguez
Born: 12 July 1991
Country: Colombia
Signed: July 2014
Appearances: 46
Goals: 17

Gareth Bale
Born: 16 July 1989
Country: Wales
Signed: September 2013
Appearances: 92
Goals: 39

Luka Modric
Born: 9 September 1985
Country: Croatia
Signed: August 2012
Appearances: 129
Goals: 7

Denis Cheryshev
Born: 26 December 1990
Country: Russia
Signed: Academy
Appearances: 1
Goals: 0

Mateo Kovacic
Born: 6 May 1994
Country: Croatia
Signed: August 2015
Appearances: 0
Goals: 0

FORWARDS

Cristiano Ronaldo
Born: 5 February 1985
Country: Portugal
Signed: June 2009
Appearances: 300
Goals: 313

Karim Benzema
Born: 19 December 1987
Country: France
Signed: July 2009
Appearances: 281
Goals: 133

Jese
Born: 26 February 1993
Country: Spain
Signed: Academy
Appearances: 56
Goals: 12

Lucas Vazquez
Born: 1 July 1991
Country: Spain
Signed: Academy
Appearances: 0
Goals: 0

Quiz Answers

P28: The BIG Real Madrid Quiz

1. 32
2. 1947
3. 61
4. Raul
5. 16.5 million
6. Atletico Madrid
7. James Bond
8. Kaka
9. Tottenham Hotspur
10. Croatia
11. Royal
12. Liverpool and Chelsea
13. Roberto Carlos, 527 games
14. 16 years and 157 days
15. Atletico Madrid
16. Adidas
17. Nine
18. Sergio Ramos
19. Five
20. Manchester United

P29: Spot the Ball answer

P40: Crossword answers

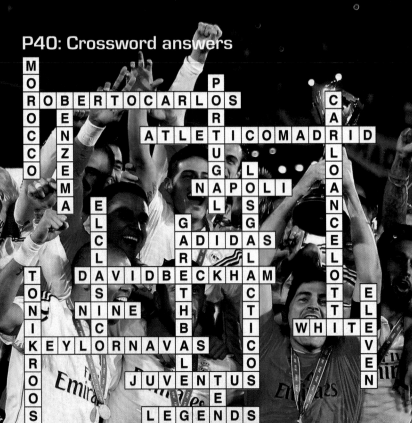

P41: Spot the difference answer

P56: True or False?

1. TRUE
2. FALSE
3. FALSE
4. TRUE
5. TRUE
6. TRUE
7. FALSE
8. TRUE
9. FALSE
10. FALSE
11. TRUE
12. TRUE
13. FALSE
14. TRUE
15. TRUE

P57: Wordsearch answers

X	C	D	T	W	S	E	T	N	E	I	R	O	M	Z	
B	E	N	Z	E	M	A	K	F	E	O	T	M	O	F	
M	D	O	B	O	K	X	R	M	L	N	N	J	R	G	
P	N	R	D	R	Q	O	B	P	S	E	A	W	A	Y	
B	H	R	O	A	D	J	W	K	A	U	Z	R	V	N	
E	I	O	Z	E	G	M	G	V	L	G	A	Y	A	B	
C	S	Q	E	R	J	L	K	G	L	A	M	G	N	V	
K	P	S	S	M	O	G	A	E	I	R	O	M	N	Q	
H	S	G	N	A	K	D	N	S	S	T	R	J	A	N	
A	A	K	A	K	N	A	R	M	A	U	A	M	C	O	
M	K	K	L	D	D	C	V	I	C	B	N	R	R	C	
L	S	G	C	I	B	R	H	K	G	G	O	R	T	R	
Q	U	G	Z	M	Z	T	L	E	M	U	E	G	Y	C	
F	P	P	U	R	D	U	A	L	Z	I	E	M	K	L	
R	O	N	A	L	D	O	N	K	H	W	P	Z	T	T	

Celyn D

PBR

A Pillar Box Red Publication

in association with

MATCH!
THE BEST FOOTBALL MAGAZINE!